Assessment of Practices in Early Elementary Classrooms (APEEC)

MARY LOUISE HEMMETER

KELLY L. MAXWELL

MELINDA JONES AULT

JOHN W. SCHUSTER

TEACHERS COLLEGE PRESS

Teachers College, Columbia University
New York and London

Published by Teachers College Press, 1234 Amsterdam Avenue, New York, NY 10027

ISBN 0-8077-4061-6

Printed on acid-free paper

Manufactured in the United States of America

13 12 11 10   5 6 7 8 9

Contents

Acknowledgments

The *Assessment of Practices in Early Elementary Classrooms* (*APEEC*) was developed through the combined efforts of numerous people, each of whom contributed from his or her specific area of expertise. We would like to thank the following people for their work, which greatly improved the quality of the finished product.

We benefited from, and are especially grateful for, the invaluable conceptual, technical, and practical advice provided by the authors of the *Early Childhood Environment Rating Scale-Revised Edition* (*ECERS-R*): Thelma Harms, Richard Clifford, and Debby Cryer. Their pioneering efforts made it easier for us to develop the *APEEC*. When creating the *APEEC*, we adopted the same basic format as the *ECERS-R*. It is important to note that neither the similar format nor the advice provided by the *ECERS-R* authors implies an endorsement of the *APEEC*.

We appreciate the thoughtful guidance provided by our colleagues on the Early Childhood Follow-Through Research Institute: Don Bailey, Carl Dunst, R. A. McWilliam, Christine Salisbury, Carol Trivette, Peg Werts, and Mark Wolery. We are especially thankful to Robin McWilliam who generously shared his knowledge of instrument validation.

The Early Childhood Follow-Through Research Institute's advisory board provided feedback throughout the development process: Ronald Anderson, Sue Bredekamp, Michael Caruso, Rose Cipollone, Richard Clifford, Carol Sue Englert, Elisabeth Healy, Bob McLaughlin, Samuel Odom, Sally Sloop, Dean Tuttle, Gary Winkler, and David Yoder. Annemarie Palincsar and Ed Blackhurst were technical consultants for the instrument.

We are grateful to the staff at the University of Kentucky for their help. Rebecca Blair Gateskill typed reviewers' comments and assisted in mailings. Dee Hill provided valuable secretarial support. William Berdine, chairperson, and Marcia Bowling , both of the Department of Special Education and Rehabilitation Counseling at the University of Kentucky, provided administrative assistance.

Several experts in early education and early childhood special education, including practitioners and researchers, reviewed the scale. Their thoughtful feedback and detailed editorial work are reflected in the final product. The reviewers included Jane Atwater, Aparna Bagdi, Jill Bartello, Ellen Bollig, Peg Burchinal, Virginia Buysse, Carey Buzelli, Lisa Campbell-Froelich, Donna Carney, Lisa Carroll, Richard Clifford, Debby Cryer, Carol Ann Davis, Ann Denney, Karen Diamond, Linda Espinosa, Sharon Esswein, Lise Fox, Lori Gillis, Ann Hains, Craig Hart, Jan Hart, Marion Hyson, Judy Jurden, Jackie Kemerer, Jean Kirshner, Frank Kohler, Susan Kontos, Mary Lynn Lewis, Joan Lieber, Anne Manning, Susan McBride, Rozanne McCall, Mary McEvoy, Margaret McKee, Mary McLean, Angela Notari-Syverson, Susan Ott, Donald Peters, Sandra Pilley, Bonney Markette Poremski, Jaipaul Rooprarine, Diane Sainato, Pat Snyder, Susan Stotts, Faith Tieszan, and Jean Trohanis.

Several people helped us collect field-test data for the instrument: from the University of Kentucky, Rebecca Blair Gateskill, Janet Hovekamp, Cynthia Pendergrast, and Kathy Watkins; from the Frank Porter Graham Child Development Center, Paulette Chetney, Syndee Kraus, Beth Partington, Canby Robinson, and Kim Sloper. We appreciate their tireless efforts and attention to detail in using multiple observation measures.

We would like to thank Brian Sullivan from the Frank Porter Graham Child Development Center, who analyzed the field-test data under the direction of Peg Burchinal.

We are most grateful for the generosity of all the teachers who allowed us to visit their classrooms. We could not have developed the *APEEC* without their assistance.

Finally, the *APEEC* was developed with support from the Early Childhood Follow-Through Research Institute, a grant funded from the U.S. Department of Education, Office of Special Education and Rehabilitation Services, Early Education Program for Children with Disabilities (Grant number HO24Q50001; Mark Wolery, Principal Investigator).

Introduction

The National Association for the Education of Young Children (NAEYC) position statement on developmentally appropriate practices (DAP) applies to children, birth through 8 years, which includes children in the primary grades (1–3) (Bredekamp & Copple, 1997). However, most measures of DAP, such as the *Early Childhood Environment Rating Scale-Revised Edition* (Harms, Clifford, & Cryer, 1998) and the *Assessment Profile for Early Childhood Programs* (Abbott-Shim & Sibley, 1988), as well as research on the concept of developmentally appropriate practices, focus on children from birth through kindergarten. Much less work has been done to understand developmentally appropriate practices in the primary grades. Even less attention has been focused on developmentally appropriate practices for school-aged children with disabilities. The *APEEC* was developed to provide a useful tool for both practitioners and researchers who want to understand elementary school practices (K–3) in general education classrooms serving children with and without disabilities. The *APEEC* does not measure specific curriculum content or in-depth teacher-child interactions. Supplemental measures should be used if these are areas of interest.

Development of the APEEC

We used a multi-step process to develop the *APEEC*. First, we reviewed the relevant literature, particularly the NAEYC guidelines and early childhood special education literature, and drew upon our professional experiences to delineate three broad domains of classroom practices: physical environment, curriculum and instruction, and social context. These three domains were used strictly as organizational categories and were not intended to be subscales. Second, we developed 40 items, formatted along a 7-point continuum with descriptors at the "1," "3," "5," and "7" anchors. Higher scores on *APEEC* items are intended to reflect higher quality classrooms, which should be associated with positive child outcomes. As the third step, we conducted a formal review of the *APEEC* by soliciting feedback from practitioners and researchers in early childhood education and early childhood special education. We invited persons serving on the boards of professional organizations and the editorial boards of several research journals to participate in the review. In addition, we asked each person to nominate outstanding teachers whom they believed operated an early elementary classroom in accordance with developmentally appropriate guidelines. These practitioners were then invited to participate in the review process.

Sixty professionals participated in the review process: 30 faculty members of universities or employees of research institutions and 30 practitioners. Overall, 46 (77%) of the professionals returned completed review materials—25 (83%) of the practitioners and 21 (70%) of the faculty members. The authors revised the *APEEC* based on the reviewers' feedback, reducing the number of items from 40 to 22. Following this revision, the development team used the measure in some classrooms. Further revisions were made based on these observations.

Fourth, we collected interrater agreement and validity data for the *APEEC* in 38 K–3 classrooms in the spring of 1997. Although the data suggested that the *APEEC* was an internally consistent, valid measure of developmentally appropriate practices, the interrater agreement data were low. Based on the 1997 field-test data, the authors revised the *APEEC*, primarily by clarifying descriptive statements on which observers disagreed frequently and shortening the number of items from 22 to 16. During the revision process, two authors pilot-tested the *APEEC* again in classrooms. As the final step, we field-tested the 16-item measure in 69 classrooms in the spring of 1998. Data from this field-test suggest that the *APEEC* is an internally consistent, valid measure of developmentally appropriate practices that has good interrater agreement.

Interrater Agreement and Validity

In the 1998 field-test of the *APEEC*, we gathered interrater agreement and validity data from 69 classrooms, grades K–3, in North Carolina and Kentucky. Overall, interrater agreement was high at the descriptor level, item level, and total score level. Interrater agreement data were available for 59 of the classrooms. At the descriptor level, the percentage of agreement among two observers across the 135 descriptors averaged 86%, with a range of 76% to 93%. At the item level, the average exact percentage of agreement was 58%, ranging from 31% to 81%, and the average percentage of agreement within 1 point was 81%, ranging from 50% to 100%. We also calculated a weighted Kappa statistic, which is a measure of reliability that accounts for chance agreement and the degree of disagreement between observers (e.g., a 1-point disagreement vs. a 4-point disagreement) (Cohen, 1968). Generally, weighted Kappas of .50 or higher are considered to be an acceptable level of agreement. On the 16 items of the *APEEC*, weighted Kappas were .50 or higher for 12 items. Of the remaining 4 items, only 2 fell below .47. The median weighted Kappa was .59. Table 1 (p. 37) presents the weighted Kappas as well as percentages for exact agreement and agreement within 1 point for each item. We also examined the internal consistency of the measure. For the total score, the intraclass correlation between the two observers' ratings was .86. In summary, these data suggest that a high level of interrater agreement can be established with the *APEEC*.

Information on the validity of the *APEEC* was gathered in 69 classrooms. Construct validity was established by comparing the *APEEC* to two other measures of developmentally appropriate practices, the *Assessment Profile for Early Childhood Programs* (Abbott-Shim & Sibley, 1988) and the *Teacher Beliefs and Practices Scale* (*TBPS*) (Buchanan, Burts, Bidner, White, & Charlesworth, 1998; Charlesworth, Hart, Burts, Thomasson, Mosley, & Fleege, 1993). We chose the *Assessment Profile for Early Childhood Programs* as a validity measure because, although it was designed to be used in preschool settings, it had recently been used in elementary grades as well. We compared the *APEEC* observation ratings to teacher perceptions of their classroom practices, using the *TBPS Developmentally Appropriate and Developmentally Inappropriate Practices scores*. We also compared the *APEEC* to a measure of teacher-child interaction, using the *Caregiver Interaction Scale* (*CIS*) (Arnett, 1989). Table 2 (p. 37) presents the Pearson correlations among these measures. The modest-to-high correlations suggest that the *APEEC* is a valid measure of developmentally appropriate practices.

Overall, the interrater agreement and validity data for the *APEEC* suggest that it is a valid, reliable tool for measuring individualized and developmentally appropriate practices in K–3 classrooms. Additional research is needed to understand further its psychometric properties.

References

Abbott-Shim, M., & Sibley, A. (1988). *Assessment Profile for Early Childhood Programs.* Atlanta, GA: Quality Assist.

Arnett, J. (1989). Caregivers in day-care centers: Does training matter? *Journal of Applied Developmental Psychology, 10*, 541–552.

Bredekamp, S., & Copple, C. (Eds.). (1997). *Developmentally appropriate practice in early childhood programs* (rev. ed.). Washington, DC: National Association for the Education of Young Children.

Buchanan, T. K., Burts, D. C., Bidner, J., White, F., & Charlesworth, R. (1998). Predictors of the developmentally appropriateness of the beliefs and practices of first, second, and third grade teachers. *Early Childhood Research Quarterly, 13*, 459–483.

Charlesworth, R., Hart, C. H., Burts, D. C., Thomasson, R. H., Mosley, J., & Fleege, P. O. (1993). Measuring the developmental appropriateness of kindergarten teachers. *Early Childhood Research Quarterly, 8*, 255–276.

Cohen, J. (1968). Weighted Kappa: Nominal scale agreement with provision for scaled disagreement or partial credit. *Psychological Bulletin, 70*, 213–220.

Harms, T., Clifford, R. M., & Cryer, D. (1998). *Early Childhood Environment Rating Scale (rev. ed.).* New York: Teachers College Press.

Instructions for Using the APEEC

To use the *APEEC* successfully, you must be knowledgeable about developmentally appropriate practices, early elementary classrooms, and special education practices. You must also familiarize yourself with the items and the score sheet and read the administration instructions below.

Setting

The *APEEC* was designed to measure practices in K–3 general education classrooms that include children with disabilities for at least part of the day. However, it may also be used in classrooms with only typically developing children. Because the *APEEC* contains items measuring practices for children with disabilities, alternative scoring instructions are given for these items if no children with disabilities are served in the classroom.

The *APEEC* was designed to measure practices in *classroom* settings. Therefore, it focuses on the arrangements and events that occur typically within the classroom itself and does not measure aspects of the broader school environment, such as the playground or special subject classes (e.g., physical education, music, art).

General Guidelines

- The field-test data for the *APEEC* were based on a one-day observation of each classroom, with a follow-up interview with the general education classroom teacher. Although it is possible to complete the *APEEC* in less than a day, we encourage you to observe as much of a full day's in-class activities as possible.
- Plan to arrive at the classroom you are rating before the children's arrival.
- Note that for each item in the *APEEC*, written descriptions (called descriptors) are provided for the "1," "3," "5," and "7" anchors along a continuum of developmentally appropriate classroom practices. For clarification, footnotes and descriptor notes are provided below some items. Read these carefully before rating descriptors as "true" or "not true."
- The methods for gathering data (i.e., observation and/or interview) are indicated in parentheses next to each item title and noted by the letter (O) for observation and (I) for interview next to each descriptor. If the descriptor has only an (O) next to it, then you must base your rating only on observation. For descriptors that indicate both observation and interview, observation data are always preferable to interview data. In other words, if you have enough observational data to make a scoring decision, do not ask an interview question.
- When you arrive in the classroom, arrange a 20–30 minute meeting with the teacher so that you may ask interview questions. It works best to conduct the interview near or at the end of the school day if possible.
- Suggested interview questions are provided on the score sheet. If you need to ask a question that is not suggested, be careful to phrase your question in an open-ended and non-leading manner.
- In many places throughout the *APEEC*, the phrase *all children* is used. When you read this phrase, score the items in terms of *all* children enrolled in the classroom, including those with disabilities.
- In some descriptors throughout the *APEEC*, the term *children* is used. When you see this term, rate the descriptor based on how it applies to *most* children in the classroom.
- In some places throughout the *APEEC*, the terms *none*, *few*, *some*, and *many* are used. Precise definitions of these terms are not provided because the definitions vary depending on the age of children and circumstances of classrooms. Use your own judgment when making these distinctions.
- In a number of descriptors and notes, we provide examples. Remember that these are only examples and everything in the examples does not have to be represented in the classroom to score the descriptor as true. In addition, other things may be

included in the classroom that do not appear in the examples that may make the descriptor true.

- Read all wordings carefully, paying particular attention to the use of *and* and *or* in a descriptor.
- Read the *APEEC* items frequently throughout the day to remind yourself of the relevant aspects of the classroom and to help you score each item.
- If a special subject teacher (e.g., music, art) teaches in the general education classroom, do not base any of your ratings on those activities.
- Use the score sheet to record your ratings of the classroom. It is permissible to copy the score sheet, but not the entire instrument. The score sheet can be used to take notes, keep a record of the activities of the day, and record answers to interview questions.

Scoring

Items are scored on a continuum of "1" to "7," which represents the extent to which developmentally appropriate practices are implemented in the classroom. For each item a score of "1" indicates the classroom is *inadequate* in terms of developmentally appropriate practices, a score of "3" indicates *minimal* developmentally appropriate practices, a score of "5" indicates the classroom is *good* in terms of developmental appropriateness, and a score of "7" indicates *excellent* developmentally appropriate practices. Intermediate scores of "2," "4," and "6" can also be obtained.

Each item's score is based on the rating of its descriptors under the anchors "1," "3," "5," and "7." To score each item, always begin by reading the descriptor(s) under "1." For each descriptor, decide whether it is true ("T"), not true ("NT"), or, in some cases, not applicable ("NA"). An observer may assign an "NA" to only those descriptors that permit it (as indicated by an "NA" on the score sheet). Descriptors that are "NA" are not used to score items. Note that, unlike the descriptors under the other anchors, the descriptors under "1" are negative and must be scored as "not true" to consider assigning a score of "3" or higher to that item.

Use the scoring rules to determine an item-level score. Begin scoring each item by reading the descriptors under anchor "1."

- If *none* of the descriptors are true (i.e., they are all "NT"), then read the descriptors under anchor "3."
- If *at least one, but not all* of the descriptors under anchor "1" are true, circle a score of "2."
- If *all* the descriptors under anchor "1" are true, circle a score of "1."

- If *none* of the anchor "3" descriptors are true (i.e., they are all "NT"), circle a score of "2."
- If *at least one, but not all* anchor "3" descriptors are true, circle a score of "2."
- If *all* of the anchor "3" descriptors are true, then read the descriptors under anchor "5."

- If *none* of the anchor "5" descriptors are true (i.e., they are all "NT"), circle a score of "3."
- If *at least one, but not all* anchor "5" descriptors are true, circle a score of "4."
- If *all* of the anchor "5" descriptors are true, then read the descriptors under anchor "7."

- If *none* of the anchor "7" descriptors are true (i.e., they are all "NT"), circle a score of "5."
- If *at least one, but not all* anchor "7" descriptors are true, circle a score of "6."
- If *all* of the anchor "7" descriptors are true, then circle a score of "7."

After a score for each item has been determined, a total *APEEC* score can be calculated by summing the item scores and dividing by the total number of items administered. This total score should exclude item 12 if it was considered not applicable ("NA").

Scoring Methods

It is possible to use two different scoring methods with the *APEEC*. The standard scoring method requires observers to rate only those descriptors required to obtain an item-level score. For example, if a score of "4" is assigned to an item, then the observer does not rate the descriptors under "7." An alternative scoring method is to use the *APEEC* as a checklist, scoring each of the 135 descriptors. This scoring method is more time-consuming and may require a longer teacher interview. However, in some cases it may be preferable because of the additional information gained.

The Score Sheet

The score sheet for the *APEEC* (see pp. 27–36) includes space for descriptor-level scores, item-level scores, and observer notes for each item. Suggested interview questions are also included for each interview item, and space is provided to record the teacher's answers. Prior to the observation, complete the identifying information on the front page of the score sheet. Write the observed classroom schedule in the space provided as the day progresses, and record the posted schedule if one is present. On the line next to each descriptor, write a "T," "NT," or "NA," using the rules described earlier in the scoring section. The numbers "1"–"7" are listed directly above the descriptors. Observers should circle the number that corresponds to the item-level score.

The standard scoring method was used in the following example. The item received a score of "4" because all of the descriptors in "1" were not true, all of the descriptors in "3" were true, and only one of the descriptors in "5" was true.

EXAMPLE:

Social Context
11. Children's Role in Decision-Making (Observation and Interview)

1	2	3	(4)	5	6	7	OBSERVATION Notes
1.1 NT 3.1 T 5.1 T 7.1 ____ 1.2 NT 3.2 T 5.2 NT 7.2 ____							Choose – seat on floor during story – partner for math game – book after finished work – learning center to do first

5.2, 7.2 Do children help make any decisions that affect the entire class or a group of children (e.g., vote, consensus)? Yes (No)

(If yes) What kinds of decisions?

How often do children make these kinds of decisions?

ITEMS OF THE

Assessment of Practices in Early Elementary Classrooms (APEEC)

Physical Environment

1. Room Arrangement
2. Display of Child Products
3. Classroom Accessibility
4. Health and Classroom Safety

Instructional Context

5. Use of Materials
6. Use of Computers
7. Monitoring Child Progress
8. Teacher-Child Language
9. Instructional Methods
10. Integration and Breadth of Subjects

Social Context

11. Children's Role in Decision-Making
12. Participation of Children with Disabilities in Classroom Activities
13. Social Skills
14. Diversity
15. Appropriate Transitions
16. Family Involvement

Physical Environment

1. Room Arrangement (Observation and Interview)

Inadequate 1	2	Minimal 3	4	Good 5	6	Excellent 7

1.1 Children use only individual desks for work (desks are separate from each other). (O)

1.2 Storage for materials^a in children's work areas is inadequate. (O)

3.1 There are at least a few soft furnishings^b in the room.* (O)

3.2 Materials^a are organized (e.g., all books are together). (O)

5.1 Children spend most of the day in small group areas.^{c} (O)

5.2 There is a relaxation area with soft furnishings.^{b}* (O)

7.1 A defined space is set aside for a child to work alone, protected from intrusion by others (with a physical boundary or a rule). Children sometimes choose when to use this space.* (O, I)

7.2 Duplicate materials^a are placed in different locations to accomplish specific tasks and activities (e.g., all materials needed to conduct, research, write about, and illustrate a science question are grouped together).* (O)

a Examples of materials: books, supplies, hands-on materials.
b Examples of soft furnishings: plush carpets, rugs, soft chairs, beanbags, pillows, other soft materials like blankets or soft toys.
c Small group areas may refer to individual desks pushed together, group tables, or areas on the floor. A small group is defined as 2–8 children.

---

*Descriptor 3.1   Regular (non-plush) floor carpeting alone is not enough to score this as "true."
*Descriptor 5.2   A relaxation area must be a clearly defined space that is at least somewhat protected by physical barriers or rules.
*Descriptor 7.1   A computer counts as a defined space only if it sits away from other computers (rather than in a row of computers) and work areas so that one child clearly has protected space.
*Descriptor 7.2   The emphasis of this item is that there are places in the room where children accomplish specific tasks and activities. All the materials necessary to accomplish the tasks are placed in that work area. Having boxes of pencils or crayons on each child's desk or at each table does not meet the intent of this descriptor.

2. Display of Child Products (Observation and Interview)

Inadequate 1	2	Minimal 3	4	Good 5	6	Excellent 7

1.1 Child products[a] are not displayed.* (O)

3.1 At least a few child products[a] are displayed. (O)

3.2 Child products are changed at least monthly. (O, I)

5.1 Some child products[a] are displayed at children's eye level.* (O)

5.2 Child products include original work (i.e., each child's project is different from the others).* (O)

5.3 Most children have at least one item displayed. (O, I)

7.1 Child products[a] include three-dimensional pieces.* (O)

7.2 Children select their items to be displayed. (I)

---

[a] Examples of child products: children's artwork, writings, papers, group projects, structures, sculptures, books produced by children.

---

*Descriptor 1.1   This descriptor is "true" if there are no child products displayed in the room. Credit is *not given* for child products displayed somewhere else in the school (e.g., hallway).

*Descriptor 5.1   To score as "true" the classroom must have some (not a few) child products displayed and at least some of the child products must be at children's eye level. If there are only a few child products displayed, then this descriptor is "not true" (no matter where they are located in the room).

*Descriptor 5.2   Artwork is considered original if the items look different or if different media are used across child projects. If the only thing different about the work is the colors used by the children, then the work is not original. For example, flowers that are the same except that children have colored them with different colors are not original. Flowers that were made with different materials (e.g., paper, cotton, glitter, felt) would be original. Written work (e.g., stories, poems) is original if each child's work is different from another.

*Descriptor 7.1   Textures on paper (e.g., buttons glued to a piece of paper) are *not* considered three-dimensional.

3. Classroom Accessibility (Observation)

Inadequate 1	2	Minimal 3	4	Good 5	6	Excellent 7
1.1 Some facilities[a] used by children are not appropriate for children's sizes.[b] (O)		3.1 Most equipment[d] used by children is appropriate for children's sizes.[e] (O)		5.1 Almost all furniture used by children is appropriate for children's sizes.[c] (O)		7.1 The room is not crowded. The room arrangement allows all children to easily move around the room (e.g., there is ample room for a walker or wheelchair to maneuver, children can go from one center to another without moving objects or squeezing through spaces). (O)
1.2 Most pieces of furniture used by children are not appropriate for children's sizes.[c] (O)		3.2 Some materials[f] can be independently accessed by children.[g] (O)		5.2 Most materials[f] can be independently accessed by children.[g] (O)		7.2 Children can independently access[g] almost all facilities,[a] equipment,[d] and materials[f] and they accommodate any special needs of children (e.g., wheelchairs fit under tables, children can transfer to equipment, children can reach paper towels).* (O)

a   Examples of facilities: toilets, sinks, water fountains. Score this item based on facilities children use (either inside or outside the classroom).

b   Examples of appropriately sized facilities: water fountains that children can use without adult assistance, sink faucets that children can use independently.

c   Examples of furniture that are appropriate for children's sizes: A chair is appropriately sized if the child fits comfortably on the seat and can place his/her feet flat on the floor when seated. Tables and desks should be at children's waist heights.

d   Equipment includes furnishings and apparatus in the classroom that support children's work or play but are not directly used by children to complete school projects. Examples of equipment: adaptive chairs, prone standers, mats, pencil sharpeners, blackboards.

e   Examples of appropriately sized equipment: pencil sharpeners that children can reach easily, adaptive equipment that is sized correctly for the child.

f   Materials are items children manipulate in order to complete their school projects. Examples of materials: books, supplies, computers, hands-on materials. Do not include materials that are packed up and stored in the classroom (e.g., box of holiday books on top of cabinet).

g   Accessibility does not include the issue of whether children have permission to obtain materials. Materials are accessible, for instance, if they are located on low shelves where children can reach them and containers can be opened independently by children. These descriptors do not apply to children whose motor ability is so limited that it prevents them from using the materials independently.

---

*Descriptor 7.2   Independent access to facilities means that the facilities are appropriate for children's sizes. If there is not a child with disabilities who requires special accommodations for facilities, equipment, furniture, or materials, consider the second part of 7.2 "NA" and rate only the first part (i.e., whether children can independently use or access almost all facilities, equipment, furniture, and materials).

4. Health and Classroom Safety (Observation and Interview)

Inadequate 1	2	Minimal 3	4	Good 5	6	Excellent 7

1.1 Health or safety problems[a] exist in the classroom. (O)

1.2 Teachers *never* provide an opportunity for children to wash their hands before eating meals or snacks. (O)

1.3 Prompts (e.g., verbal reminders or posters in bathroom) to wash hands after toileting are *not* provided.* (O)

3.1 Basic first aid equipment (i.e., band-aids, disposable latex gloves) is present in the classroom. (I)

3.2 Children's medical and emergency information is readily available in the classroom (e.g., information on children's allergies, seizures, emergency contact persons, telephone numbers). (I)

5.1 There is a working two-way communication system between the classroom and other adults in the school (e.g., telephone, two-way intercom system with the office). (O, I)

5.2 Teachers provide an opportunity for children to wash their hands before eating meals *and* snacks.* (O)

7.1 Special precautions are taken for children with disabilities (e.g., wheel-chair accessibility to exit door, safe storage area for crutches or walkers, pathways free of clutter).* (O, I)

7.2 First aid and crisis information are in the classroom (e.g., posters on walls, cards/booklets containing procedures for specific emergencies associated with the special needs of the children such as seizures, choking, shunt malfunction). (I)

7.3 One member of the classroom staff is certified in first aid *and* CPR procedures. (I)

---

a Examples of health or safety problems: unstable furniture, medicines not locked away or out of reach, toxic chemicals not labeled and not properly stored (chemicals should always be labeled but it is more important that they be out of reach for younger children than for older children), obstructed exits, rabbit cage next to children's food, cockroaches present, a hot coffeepot in children's work area.

---

*Descriptor 1.3   Score as "not true" if children consistently wash their hands without prompts.
*Descriptor 5.2   If snacks are not provided, then score this item according to what happens at mealtimes.
*Descriptor 7.1   Score as "NA" if no children in the classroom have physical disabilities or health problems that require special attention (e.g., diabetes).

Instructional Context

5. Use of Materials (Observation and Interview)

Inadequate 1	2	Minimal 3	4	Good 5	6	Excellent 7

1.1 Minimal hands-on materials[a] are in the classroom. (O)

1.2 All activities are paper and pencil tasks. (O)

3.1 Hands-on materials[a] are used in at least one subject area to appropriately support child learning.[b]* (O)

3.2 The teacher ensures that children use materials properly (e.g., teacher shows children how to use a microscope, helps children learn rules of game, reminds children of proper use).* (O)

5.1 Many different hands-on materials[a] in at least two subject areas are in the classroom. (O)

5.2 Hands-on materials or other relevant materials[c] are used by most children in at least two subject areas to appropriately support child learning.[b] (O)

7.1 All children use hands-on materials[a] for a majority of the day. (O)

7.2 Hands-on and other relevant materials[c] are used by most children in all subject areas to appropriately support child learning.[b]* (O, I)

---

a Examples of hands-on materials: art supplies, games, coins, blocks, unifix cubes, scales, three-dimensional shapes, counters, rulers, puppets, plants.

b Examples of how materials are used to support child learning: math cubes used for solving math problems, art materials used for creativity, scales used for testing hypotheses about weights of objects, blocks and interlocking pieces to learn basic building and physics concepts, math games to teach relevant math concepts, and live animals and plants to teach growth. Because different materials may be needed to support some children's learning (e.g., children with lower-level math skills need less difficult math games), look for materials at various skill levels. To be considered as supporting children's learning, teachers should redirect children to more appropriate materials if they are using an inappropriate material; or there is evidence in the lesson plans that the materials used were selected for a specific purpose.

c Other relevant materials include a variety of children's books (e.g., children's literature, library books, fiction and non-fiction books) and paper and pencil when they are used to foster activities about children's real-life experiences (e.g., teaching writing skills by asking children to write creative stories, make journal entries, or write poetry as opposed to copying sentences).

---

*Descriptor 3.1   Score as "true" even if only a few children use hands-on learning materials.

*Descriptor 3.2   Score as "true" if children are using materials properly, even without teacher intervention. Score as "not true" if children never use hands-on materials.

*Descriptor 7.2   All subject areas include math, language arts, science, and social studies. To score this descriptor as "true," the teacher must give at least two examples of children's use of materials in each subject area.

6. Use of Computers (Observation and Interview)

Inadequate 1	2	Minimal 3	4	Good 5	6	Excellent 7

1.1 The computer(s) in the school is used by the class less than once a week or is not available to the class. (O, I)

3.1 The computer(s) is used by the class at least twice a week. (O, I)

3.2 Some computer programs that are being used either in the classroom or in a computer lab relate to classroom activities (e.g., math drill and practice, reading program, word processing). (O, I)

5.1 The classroom has at least two computers that children use. (O)

5.2 Children use computers for at least three purposes (e.g., reinforcing a skill, word processing, teaching a new skill, drawing). (O, I)

7.1 Children use the Internet at school.* (O, I)

7.2 Children use computers for research purposes (e.g., CD-ROM encyclopedia, Internet).* (O, I)

---

*Descriptor 7.1, 7.2 Children can work alone or in a group when using computers for Internet or research purposes. Score this descriptor as "true" if children use any school computer for Internet or research purposes (it does not have to happen in the classroom). In kindergarten or first grade, looking up words on a computer dictionary or observing while an adult uses a CD-ROM encyclopedia meets the criterion for using computers for research purposes. In kindergarten and first grade, it is also acceptable for children to observe while an adult works on the Internet. To score this descriptor as "true" for second and third graders, the children must work on the computers themselves (although an adult may be supervising their work).

7. Monitoring Child Progress (Interview)

Inadequate 1	2	Minimal 3	4	Good 5	6	Excellent 7

1.1 The teacher evaluates children primarily through grades. (I)

3.1 At least 2 types of data,^{a} besides test or worksheet grades, are used to monitor children's progress. (I)

3.2 Data on children's progress are collected at least once a month. (I)

5.1 Data^a on individual child progress are used to make instructional decisions.^{b} (I)

5.2 The teacher collects data on IEP objectives^c at least quarterly or at report card times.* (I)

7.1 Data^a on children's progress are collected primarily within the context of instruction at least once every 2 weeks through written records *and* collection of permanent products or projects. (I)

7.2 The teacher collects data on IEP objectives^c at least every 2 weeks.* (I)

7.3 The teacher formally schedules a conference with each child at least once a grading period to review his or her overall progress over time.(I)

---

a Data include any type of written record or collection of permanent products. Written records include teacher notes (e.g., teacher diary, anecdotal records), individually administered assessments, checklists (e.g., teacher-made skill lists), tally marks on an index card, and so forth. Permanent products include creative writing samples, artwork, or final products of group projects.

b Examples of how data are used to make instructional decisions: selecting activities, placing children in groups, modifying materials, deciding to teach a new skill, deciding to continue working on a skill.

c IEP objectives are the short-term instructional objectives written on the child's current Individual Education Program.

---

*Descriptor 5.2, 7.2   Score this descriptor as "true" only if general education teachers or their assistants collect the data on IEP objectives. Data must include information about children's progress on IEP objectives. However, the data collection system does not have to be different from the system used for other children, as long as the system enables the teacher to monitor children's progress on IEP objectives. For example, if a teacher records notes on each child's reading skills during a weekly one-on-one reading lesson, this may be an appropriate system for monitoring the progress of an IEP objective related to reading. If the teacher does not know the child's IEP objectives, score this as "not true." Score as "NA" if no children in the classroom have IEPs.

8. Teacher-Child Language (Observation)

Inadequate		Minimal		Good		Excellent
1	2	3	4	5	6	7

1.1 Almost all teacher questions have one correct answer or require rote memorization of facts. (O)

1.2 Almost all child language is teacher-directed (e.g., teacher chooses topic, children speak primarily in response to teacher). (O)

3.1 Teacher shows interest in children's statements or questions. (O)

3.2 The teacher's feedback to children is constructive, not critical. (O)

3.3 Children have some opportunities to talk with their peers about classroom activities. (O)

5.1 Some teacher questions require something other than one correct answer or rote memorization of facts.[a] (O)

5.2 At least a few times a day, the teacher prompts children to elaborate[b] on their initial statements. (O)

5.3 Children have many opportunities to talk with their peers about classroom activities. (O)

7.1 Many times a day, the teacher prompts children to elaborate[b] on their initial statements. (O)

7.2 The teacher has some informal conversations[c] with children. (O)

[a] Examples of teacher questions requiring more than one correct answer: What do you think will happen next? How could you solve this problem? What are some ways we can add numbers to make 10? What words start with the letter L? If you lived in 1900, what would your life have been like?

[b] Elaboration requires the teacher to ask follow-up questions of a child to elicit additional statements from him or her. Asking multiple questions to a group of children is not considered elaboration. Examples of elaborations: Teacher: What is the answer to this question? Child: 4. Teacher: How did you know that?; Teacher: What did Joe do next in the story? Child: He ran away. Teacher: Why do you think he ran away?

[c] A conversation is not simply asking and answering a question, giving directions, or clarifying a task.

9. Instructional Methods (Observation)

Inadequate 1	2	Minimal 3	4	Good 5	6	Excellent 7
1.1 Whole group instruction is used all day. (O)		*3.1* The teacher uses at least two different teaching methods.[a] (O) *3.2* Some activities or materials are adapted[b] for individual children as needed.* (O)		*5.1* Shared learning[a] is used at least once a day. (O) *5.2* Most activities or materials are adapted[b] for individual children as needed.* (O) *5.3* The teacher asks children to explain their answers at least a few times a day.* (O)		*7.1* The teacher uses at least two teaching methods within at least two subject areas.[a] (O) *7.2* The teacher facilitates group discussions[c] among children. (O)

a Teaching methods include *whole group instruction* (e.g., lecturing, giving directions, giving feedback to children during teacher-directed activities in which all children are working on the same thing, demonstrating new tasks in a large group setting), *small group instruction* (e.g., teacher-led reading groups), *one-on-one instruction* (e.g., teacher works with an individual child), *self-instruction* (e.g., children directing their own play with materials, reading alone, working on an educational computer program), *teacher facilitation* (e.g., teacher expands on child-directed activities), and *shared learning* in which children work together to complete an activity (e.g., cooperative learning, games, peer tutoring).

b Examples of material and activity adaptations: alternate keyboards for children with physical disabilities, reading materials available for children at different reading levels, large print materials for children with visual impairments, shorter assignments for children with developmental delays, peer assistance, ability-based reading groups, materials available in children's primary language.

c Group discussions go beyond the teacher asking and children answering questions. In group discussions, children present their opinions, consider different issues of a problem, talk about pros and cons, and so forth. No one person (e.g., teacher, child) is the primary source of information during group discussions. Group discussions may be among the whole class or a smaller group of children.

---

*Descriptor 3.2, 5.2 This item is based on observation only. Pay attention to the number of materials that are adapted as needed. It is not enough to adapt just one material if, in fact, several need to be adapted. Also remember that adaptations need to be made for any child whose skills are above or below the level required by the material, not just children with disabilities. Ability-based groups should be considered as an adapted activity.

*Descriptor 5.3 Remember that asking for an explanation is always an elaboration, but elaborations are not always explanations.

10. Integration and Breadth of Subjects (Observation and Interview)

Inadequate		Minimal		Good		Excellent
1	2	3	4	5	6	7

1.1 The day is divided into subject areas, with each area taught only during its allotted time slot, and there is no common content across subject areas.* (O)

3.1 Fine arts[a] are offered at least twice a week. At least one of these times must be in the classroom. (O, I)

3.2 Math and language arts[b] and either science *or* social studies are taught at least weekly. (O, I)

5.1 Activities or projects that require children to use skills from multiple-subject areas concurrently are used at least once a day.* (O)

5.2 Math, language arts,[b] science, *and* social studies are taught at least weekly in the classroom. (I)

5.3 Opportunities for gross-motor activities are provided daily for all children.* (I)

7.1 At least half of the classroom time is organized by activities or projects that require children to use skills from multiple-subject areas concurrently.* (O)

7.2 Math, science, social studies, and language arts[b] are taught at least twice a week. Each subject must be taught at least once a week in the classroom. (I)

[a] Fine arts includes drama, art (e.g., painting, drawing, sculpture), dance, and music.
[b] Language arts includes reading, creative writing, spelling, grammar, and public speaking.

---

*Descriptor 1.1 When rating this descriptor, exclude calendar/circle time.

*Descriptor 5.1, 7.1 Activities that occur within circle/calendar time do not count unless an individual activity uses two skills concurrently. Moving quickly from a science activity (e.g., what's the weather today) to a math activity (e.g., how many days are left in the month) does not count because each activity requires only one skill. If a child reads the instructions of a math worksheet, that does not count as an activity requiring skills from multiple subject areas. Almost every school activity requires some reading (e.g., reading instructions on a math worksheet). More extensive reading is necessary to consider an activity as requiring reading skills. An example of using multiple-skill areas concurrently is a project on bees in which children have to do research in the library or on a computer, estimate the number of bees in a hive, and write a report.

*Descriptor 5.3 All children must have a daily opportunity for gross-motor activities somewhere inside or outside the school, even in bad weather. If the teacher routinely keeps children inside from recess to finish their work (and recess is the only gross motor activity that day) or children participate in passive activities such as playing board games when the weather is inclement, then this criterion has not been met.

Social Context

11. Children's Role in Decision-Making (Observation and Interview)

Inadequate 1	2	Minimal 3	4	Good 5	6	Excellent 7

1.1 Children never make choices[a] about their classroom activities. (O)

1.2 Children never choose whom they sit by, work with, or play with in the classroom. (O)

3.1 Children make choices[a] in the classroom at least twice a day. (O)

3.2 Children choose whom they sit by, work with, or play with in the classroom at least twice a day. (O)

5.1 At least once a day, children decide which activity to do (e.g., choose an activity in a center, decide between writing or playing a math game).* (O)

5.2 Children help make at least three different decisions that affect the entire class or a group of children in the class.[b] (O, I)

7.1 Children make choices[a] many times a day. (O)

7.2 Children help make decisions[b] at least once a month that affect the entire class or a group of children in the class. (I)

a Child choice may include choices between activities (e.g., whether to draw a picture or read a book) or between teacher-identified options (e.g., children must write a story, but they can decide the topic; children can select a math game to play or a book to read after completing work).

b The intent of this is for children to make decisions together. Do not include decisions that one child makes that may affect the entire class or group of children (e.g., one child is allowed to choose four friends to sit with at lunch). Examples of decisions made by a group: class rules, topics of study, field trips, books to be read aloud, projects to complete, games to play.

---

*Descriptor 5.1   This does not include choosing "filler" activities until it is time to move to the next major activity.

12. Participation of Children with Disabilities in Classroom Activities (Observation and Interview) **

Inadequate 1	2	Minimal 3	4	Good 5	6	Excellent 7
1.1 The general education teacher does not know the IEP objectives[a] for each child with disabilities in the class.* (I) 1.2 At least one child with disabilities rarely participates in the same classroom activities[b] as the children without disabilities.* (O)		3.1 The general education teacher communicates with other educational team members[c] about child progress (not including report cards or annual IEP meetings). (I) 3.2 All children with disabilities participate in many of the same classroom activities[b] as the children without disabilities.* (O)		5.1 Some IEP objectives[a] are addressed within the context of regular classroom activities.[b]* (I) 5.2 All children with disabilities participate in almost all of the same classroom activities, with appropriate modifications, as the children without disabilities.* (O)		7.1 Many IEP objectives[a] for children with disabilities are addressed through regular classroom activities[b] (e.g., a child with disabilities is not pulled out of an activity to do something different).* (I) 7.2 The general education teacher has an ongoing, formal collaborative relationship with other educational team members[c] about children with disabilities.* (I)

[a] IEP objectives are the short-term instructional objectives written on the child's current Individual Education Program.

[b] Classroom activities are those in which the typically developing children in the class are participating. These activities can be modified to meet the needs of the child with disabilities. This does not necessarily imply that children with disabilities are learning the same content as children without disabilities. Different skills may be taught within the same activities.

[c] Examples of educational team members: special educators, paraprofessionals, speech-language pathologists, psychologists, occupational therapists, physical therapists, art teachers, music teachers, physical education teachers.

** Score this item and all descriptors as "NA" if no children with disabilities are included in the classroom.

*Descriptor 1.1   Score this as "not true" only if the teacher provides specific examples of IEP objectives. Describing the general subject areas, like math or reading, does not meet the criterion for this descriptor. The teacher must know the IEP objectives for all children with disabilities in the class.

*Descriptor 1.2,   Score this based on what happens when the child is in the general education classroom, even if the child spends minimal time in this class.
3.2, 5.2

*Descriptor 5.1,   Score this as "true" if either the general educator or specialist address IEP objectives through regular class activities.
7.1

*Descriptor 7.2   Score this as "true" only if the teacher has a *formal*, collaborative relationship with other team members such as holding regular meetings with professionals at least once a month, joint teaching, or sharing responsibilities for planning.

13. Social Skills (Observation)

Inadequate 1	2	Minimal 3	4	Good 5	6	Excellent 7
1.1 Adults[a] predominately use a hostile tone when managing class behavior (e.g., criticize, scold, speak sarcastically, yell). (O) 1.2 At least one child primarily receives adult attention for negative behavior only (e.g., teacher repeatedly scolds a child, but never praises him or her).* (O)		3.1 Adults[a] frequently demonstrate positive social skills[b] throughout the day.* (O) 3.2 Adults occasionally praise children for appropriate social behavior.* (O) 3.3 Rules for appropriate behavior are posted in the room. (O)		5.1 Adults[a] primarily use redirection or reinforcement of appropriate behavior to minimize inappropriate behavior. (O) 5.2 Adults' expectations of children's behavior are appropriate for children's ages and abilities.[c] (O) 5.3 Consequences for inappropriate behavior are implemented consistently (or consequences are not necessary). (O)		7.1 Adults[a] encourage positive social interactions among children (e.g., discuss good character traits, facilitate sharing between children).* (O) 7.2 Adults encourage children to negotiate their own solutions to problems (e.g., poster on wall about problem solving, teachers remind children about negotiating conflicts, designated space in classroom for resolving conflicts).* (O)

a   Adults include teachers, assistants, and other paid staff in the classroom.

b   Examples of positive social skills: smiling, comforting others, expressing feelings appropriately, getting along with others, using good manners.

c   Examples of appropriate adult expectations: allowing children to talk, involving children in active activities, having individualized expectations for children based on their level of functioning.

---

*Descriptor 1.2   If you notice the adults primarily providing negative attention to a child (who may have problem behaviors), then pay close attention to determine if negative attention is the only type of attention received by this child (i.e., the teacher rarely attends to the positive behavior of the child). If it is, then the descriptor should be scored as "true."

*Descriptor 3.1   This descriptor means that the adults, in general, interact with children in a courteous and respectful manner during most of the day.

*Descriptor 3.2   Appropriate social behavior includes behaviors other than academic responses. For example, raising hands, waiting turns, helping a child, picking up a book someone dropped, sharing with others, and solving conflicts constructively are appropriate social behaviors versus correct answers to teacher questions.

*Descriptor 7.1   Adults must encourage positive social interactions in the absence of problems. If adults encourage positive social interactions only when there is a problem between children, this indicator should be scored "not true."

*Descriptor 7.2   If problems between children are not observed, written evidence of a plan or strategies must be present in the room.

14. Diversity (Observation and Interview)

Inadequate 1	2	Minimal 3	4	Good 5	6	Excellent 7
1.1 The teacher communicates a biased perspective^a through statements, displays, or activities. (O)		*3.1* Some materials or information^b on diversity are present in the classroom. (O)		*5.1* A variety of materials and information^b on diversity are present in the classroom.* (O)		*7.1* Diversity in the classroom is seen across multiple areas.^{c} (O)
		3.2 Diversity information is discussed at least twice a year (e.g., at holidays, in special unit). (I)		*5.2* Diversity information is provided through ongoing areas of study, information provided by the teacher, or activities.* (I)		*7.2* Diversity information^b is integrated throughout daily activities. (O, I)

^{a} Examples of a biased perspective: teacher says "sit Indian style," sings church songs, has posters related to only one religion displayed (e.g., picture of Santa Claus without pictures relating to other religious holidays for the month of December), only assigns girls to the housekeeping center.

^{b} Examples of materials and information: books, displays, activities, music.

^{c} Examples of areas of diversity: gender, disability, family configurations, languages/cultures.

---

*Descriptor 5.1   For 5.1 to be "true," diversity must be represented in more than just books and pictures on the wall.

*Descriptor 5.2   Diversity is taught as part of ongoing activities, not as a separate unit on diversity. It is embedded into activities.

15. Appropriate Transitions (Observation and Interview)

Inadequate		Minimal		Good		Excellent
1	**2**	**3**	**4**	**5**	**6**	**7**

1.1 Children spend time between activities waiting without having something to do.* (O)

1.2 Children are not given extra in-class time to complete any activities.* (O, I)

3.1 Most of the transitions between activities occur in an orderly fashion.* (O)

3.2 For some activities, children are allowed to begin another activity while waiting for others to finish (e.g., read a book). (O, I)

5.1 The teacher provides advance notice about most upcoming transitions, including those in which the children will be moving outside of the classroom. (O)

5.2 Children are almost always allowed to begin another activity when finished with an activity. (O, I)

7.1 At least once a day, children move independently from one scheduled activity to another, in small groups or individually.* (O)

7.2 Children are allowed to spend extra in-class time to complete all activities. Extra time must be provided within a day from when children began the activity.* (I)

---

*Descriptor 1.1   For this to be "true," children must wait between almost all activities.

*Descriptor 1.2   Score this on the basis of what happens for most children. If the teacher provides extra in-class time but it is punitive in nature, then 1.2 is "true." For example, extra in-class time must not be during recess or in place of a special activity (like Friday fun time).

*Descriptor 3.1   An orderly transition does not mean children have to be quiet or stand in line, rather the transition is completed quickly and with some order. A disorderly transition looks chaotic. For example, children may run around the room, throw objects, or yell.

*Descriptor 7.1   Score this on the basis of what happens for most children. Consider only those transitions that occur within the classroom or between the classroom and the bathroom. Do not consider transitions from the classroom to art, music, physical education, computer lab, library, assemblies, lunch. An example of moving independently from one scheduled activity to another is that when children finish their math project, they begin their social studies research project. If children move among multiple centers during center time, then each center is considered a "scheduled activity" and transitions from center to center should be scored.

*Descriptor 7.2   Extra time to complete the unfinished activity must be given the same day, or the day after, children started working on the activity.

16. Family Involvement (Observation and Interview)

Inadequate 1	2	Minimal 3	4	Good 5	6	Excellent 7

1.1 The teacher does not communicate with families except when initiated by the family members. (I)

1.2 Families are given only a few options to participate in the classroom, such as bringing treats or chaperoning trips. (I)

3.1 The teacher communicates with families at least twice each grading period, through individualized^a or mass communication.^{b} (O, I)

3.2 The teacher offers family conferences at least twice a year. (I)

3.3 Families have a standing invitation from the teacher to visit the classroom. (I)

5.1 A communication system is present so that families and teachers can communicate easily and in a timely manner (e.g., daily communication notebooks, teacher provides home telephone number, voice mail, phone in classroom, e-mail). (O, I)

5.2 Families are given a variety of options for involvement in classroom-related activities (e.g., observation, tutors, clerical workers, guest speakers, material preparation, selecting curriculum, field trips, parties in the classroom). (I)

5.3 The teacher has met the parent, guardian, or primary caregiver of all children. (I)

7.1 The teacher communicates with families at least once a month concerning each child's overall progress at school. (O, I)

7.2 The school or teacher asks families how they want to be involved in classroom-related activities.* (I)

7.3 The school or teacher asks families to evaluate their child's classroom, school, or teacher at least annually. (I)

---

^{a} Examples of individualized communication: conferences, home visits, e-mail messages, telephone calls.
^{b} Examples of mass communication: classroom newsletters, event calendars.

---

*Descriptor 7.2   Parents must be given the opportunity to offer their own ideas for involvement.

SCORE SHEET FOR THE

Assessment of Practices in Early Elementary Classrooms (APEEC)

Assessment of Practices in Early Elementary Classrooms (APEEC)
Score Sheet

Mary Louise Hemmeter, Kelly L. Maxwell, Melinda Jones Ault, and John W. Schuster

Date _____   Observer's Name _____   Teacher _____   School _____   Grade _____

Arrival Time _____   Departure Time _____   Number of Children Present _____   Number of Children with Disabilities _____

Classroom Schedule	Notes

Physical Environment

1. Room Arrangement (Observation and Interview)

1	2	3	4	5	6	7		OBSERVATION Notes

1.1 _____   3.1 _____   5.1 _____   7.1 _____

1.2 _____   3.2 _____   5.2 _____   7.2 _____

7.1 When are children allowed to use a defined space to work alone?

2. Display of Child Products (Observation and Interview)

1	2	3	4	5	6	7		OBSERVATION Notes

1.1 _____   3.1 _____   5.1 _____   7.1 _____

            3.2 _____   5.2 _____   7.2 _____

                                 5.3 _____

3.2 How often do you change the display of children's work?

5.3, 7.2 How are the pieces of children's work selected for display?

3. Classroom Accessibility (Observation)

	1	2	3	4	5	6	7		OBSERVATION Notes

1.1 _____   3.1 _____   5.1 _____   7.1 _____

1.2 _____   3.2 _____   5.2 _____   7.2 _____

4. Health and Classroom Safety (Observation and Interview)

	1	2	3	4	5	6	7		OBSERVATION Notes

1.1 _____   3.1 _____   5.1 _____   7.1 _____NA

1.2 _____   3.2 _____   5.2 _____   7.2 _____

1.3 _____   7.3 _____

3.1 Do you have first aid equipment in the room?   Yes   No
   (If yes) Describe the equipment you keep in the room.

5.1 Is there a phone in the classroom?   Yes   No
   (If no) Is there a working two-way intercom system in the
   classroom?   Yes   No

7.2 Do you keep first aid manuals or information in the room?   Yes   No

3.2 Where is children's medical and emergency information kept?

7.1 What safety precautions do you take specifically related to children with disabilities?

7.3 Are you or your assistant certified in first aid?   Yes   No   CPR?

Instructional Context

5. Use of Materials (Observation and Interview)

	1	2	3	4	5	6	7		OBSERVATION Notes

1.1 _____   3.1 _____   5.1 _____   7.1 _____

1.2 _____   3.2 _____   5.2 _____   7.2 _____

7.2 What kinds of things do you do in math?

    In language arts?

    In science?

    In social studies?

6. Use of Computers (Observation and Interview)

	1	2	3	4	5	6	7		OBSERVATION Notes

1.1 _____   3.1 _____   5.1 _____   7.1 _____

              3.2 _____   5.2 _____   7.2 _____

1.1, 3.1 How often do children use computers?

7.1 Do children use the Internet?   Yes   No

3.2, 5.2, 7.2 What kinds of things do children do on the computers?

7. Monitoring Child Progress (Interview)

	1	2	3	4	5	6	7

OBSERVATION Notes

1.1 _____   3.1 _____   5.1 _____   7.1 _____

3.2 _____   5.2 _____ NA   7.2 _____ NA

7.3 _____

1.1, 3.1, 7.1 How do you evaluate children's work and progress?

3.2, 7.1 How often do you evaluate work and progress?

5.2, 7.2 Do you keep track of children's progress on IEP objectives?

Yes   No

(If yes) How often do you collect data on IEP objectives?

(If no) Is that the special educator's responsibility?

Yes   No

3.1, 5.1 What are all the ways you use the information you collect?

7.3 Do you have formal conferences with children like you do with parents?   Yes   No

(If yes) How often do you have the conferences?

What do you discuss?

8. Teacher-Child Language (Observation)

	1	2	3	4	5	6	7

OBSERVATION Notes

1.1 _____   3.1 _____   5.1 _____   7.1 _____

1.2 _____   3.2 _____   5.2 _____   7.2 _____

3.3 _____   5.3 _____

9. Instructional Methods (Observation)

	1	2	3	4	5	6	7		*OBSERVATION Notes*

1.1 _____   3.1 _____   5.1 _____   7.1 _____

　　　　　　　　　　 3.2 _____   5.2 _____   7.2 _____

　　　　　　　　　　　　　　　　　　　 5.3 _____

10. Integration and Breadth of Subjects (Observation and Interview)

	1	2	3	4	5	6	7		*OBSERVATION Notes*

1.1 _____   3.1 _____   5.1 _____   7.1 _____

　　　　　　　　　　 3.2 _____   5.2 _____   7.2 _____

　　　　　　　　　　　　　　　　　　　 5.3 _____

3.1 Do you cover fine arts in the classroom?   Yes   No

(If yes) How often?

5.3 How often do children have physical education?

*5.3 What do you do when it is bad weather and you can't go
outside for recess?*

3.2, 5.2, 7.2 How often do you cover math?

Language arts?

Science?

Social studies?

Social Context

11. Children's Role in Decision-Making (Observation and Interview)

	1	2	3	4	5	6	7	OBSERVATION Notes

1.1 _____   3.1 _____   5.1 _____   7.1 _____

1.2 _____   3.2 _____   5.2 _____   7.2 _____

5.2, 7.2 Do children help make any decisions that affect the entire class or a group of children (e.g., vote, consensus)?   Yes   No

(If yes) What kinds of decisions?

How often do children make these kinds of decisions?

12. Participation of Children with Disabilities in Classroom Activities (Observation and Interview)

	1	2	3	4	5	6	7	NA	OBSERVATION Notes

1.1 _____   3.1 _____   5.1 _____   7.1 _____

1.2 _____   3.2 _____   5.2 _____   7.2 _____

1.1 Do you know the specific IEP objectives for all of the children in your class who have IEPs?   Yes   No

5.1, 7.1 (If yes) Do you or a specialist address any of the IEP objectives in class?   Yes   No

(If yes) How many objectives do you address?

3.1 Do you communicate with other members of this child's (children's) educational team?   Yes   No

(If yes) What kinds of things do you discuss?

7.2 How do you work together with the other team members?

13. Social Skills (Observation)

	1	2	3	4	5	6	7		OBSERVATION Notes

1.1 _____   3.1 _____   5.1 _____   7.1 _____

1.2 _____   3.2 _____   5.2 _____   7.2 _____

               3.3 _____   5.3 _____

14. Diversity (Observation and Interview)

	1	2	3	4	5	6	7		OBSERVATION Notes

1.1 _____   3.1 _____   5.1 _____   7.1 _____

               3.2 _____   5.2 _____   7.2 _____

3.2, 5.2, 7.2 How do you address multicultural or other diversity issues?

15. Appropriate Transitions (Observation and Interview)

1	2	3	4	5	6	7	OBSERVATION Notes

1.1 _____   3.1 _____   5.1 _____   7.1 _____

1.2 _____   3.2 _____   5.2 _____   7.2 _____

1.2, 7.2 What happens if a child does not finish something during the time you have allotted?

3.2, 5.2 What happens if a child finishes something early?

16. Family Involvement (Observation and Interview)

1	2	3	4	5	6	7	OBSERVATION Notes

1.1 _____   3.1 _____   5.1 _____   7.1 _____

1.2 _____   3.2 _____   5.2 _____   7.2 _____

            3.3 _____   5.3 _____   7.3 _____

1.1, 3.1, 5.1, 7.1 How do you communicate with families?

        How often do you communicate with families?

3.2 Do you have family conferences?   Yes   No
   (If yes) How often?

5.1 Is there a phone in the classroom?   Yes   No
   (If no) How do families get in touch with you?

7.1 What are the ways you communicate with families about their child's progress?

        How often do you communicate about progress?

1.2, 5.2 Are there opportunities for families to be involved in the class?   Yes   No
   (If yes) What kinds?

3.3 Can families visit the classroom?   Yes   No
   (If yes) When?

5.3 Have you met all the parents?   Yes   No

7.2 How do you decide what kinds of classroom-related activities parents can do?

7.3 Are parents ever asked to evaluate the school, class, or teacher?   Yes   No
   (If yes) How often?

APEEC Summary Score Sheet

Instructions: This summary sheet is for use with the standard scoring method. Use this sheet to summarize the item-level scores and calculate the total *APEEC* score.

1.   Transfer each item-level score from the score sheet to the corresponding lines below.
2.   Add all item-level scores and enter the sum on the corresponding line.
3.   Enter the total number of items scored on the corresponding line.
4.   Calculate the total *APEEC* score by dividing the sum of the item-level scores (line 2) by the total number of items scored (line 3) and enter the quotient on the corresponding line.

1. ITEM-LEVEL SCORES

Physical Environment
1. _____
2. _____
3. _____
4. _____

2. Sum of item-level scores = _____

3. Total number of items scored = _____

Instructional Context
5. _____
6. _____
7. _____
8. _____
9. _____
10. _____

4. TOTAL *APEEC* SCORE = _____

Social Context
11. _____
12. _____
13. _____
14. _____
15. _____
16. _____

TABLE 1. *Interrater Agreement Data for Each Item of the APEEC*

Item	% Exact Agreement (N = 59)	% Agreement within 1 point (N = 59)	Weighted Kappa (N = 59)
1. Room arrangement	59	78	.62
2. Display of child products	61	86	.67
3. Classroom accessibility	36	75	.39
4. Health and classroom safety	86	95	.78
5. Use of materials	41	75	.53
6. Use of computers	66	85	.68
7. Monitoring child progress	53	78	.47
8. Teacher-child language	39	73	.48
9. Instructional methods	68	86	.67
10. Integration and breadth of subjects	63	85	.61
11. Children's role in decision-making	63	90	.72
12. Participation of children with disabilities in classroom activities	58	80	.55
13. Social skills	58	73	.58
14. Diversity	63	83	.58
15. Appropriate transitions	41	69	.41
16. Family involvement	71	80	.66

TABLE 2. *Pearson Correlations Between the APEEC and Other Measures of Developmentally Appropriate Practices*

Measures	Assessment Profile for Early Childhood Programs (N = 69)	TBPS Developmentally Appropriate Practices (N = 68)	TBPS Developmentally Inappropriate Practices (N = 68)	Caregiver Interaction Scale (N = 61)
APEEC	.67	.55	-.28	.61

About the Authors

Mary Louise Hemmeter is currently an Associate Professor in the Department of Special Education and Rehabilitation Counseling at the University of Kentucky. As of August 2001, she will be an Associate Professor in the Department of Special Education at the University of Illinois at Urbana-Champaign. Dr. Hemmeter received her undergraduate degree at Auburn University in Early Childhood and Special Education. She received her M.Ed. in Early Childhood Special Education and her Ph.D. in Education and Human Development from Vanderbilt University. She is past president of the Council for Exceptional Children's Division for Early Childhood. Her research interests include effective instruction in early childhood and early elementary classrooms, language development and intervention, and evaluation of early childhood and primary programs.

Kelly Maxwell is a Research Investigator at the Frank Porter Graham Child Development Center, University of North Carolina at Chapel Hill. She is also a Clinical Assistant Professor in the School of Education at the University of North Carolina at Chapel Hill. Dr. Maxwell received her undergraduate degree in Psychology from Illinois State University in 1986 and received her Doctorate in School Psychology from the University of North Carolina at Chapel Hill in 1993. Her professional interests include individualized and developmentally appropriate practices in preschool and the early elementary grades, school readiness, and evaluation of early childhood initiatives.

Melinda Jones Ault is currently a research associate in the Department of Special Education and Rehabilitation Counseling at the University of Kentucky. She received her bachelor's and master's degrees from the University of Kentucky in elementary and special education. She is a certified elementary education and special education teacher, was a former classroom teacher, and has worked in educational research for 15 years. Ms. Ault is co-author of a textbook on instructional strategies for students with moderate to severe disabilities. Her research interests are instructional methodology for persons with severe disabilities and the inclusion of students with disabilities into general education classrooms.

John W. Schuster is currently Professor and Director of Graduate Studies in the Department of Special Education and Rehabilitation Counseling at the University of Kentucky. He received his bachelor's degree from the University of Alabama, his master's degree from Teachers College, Columbia University, and earned his doctorate from the University of Kentucky in 1987. His research interests include effective and efficient instructional methodology for students with disabilities, distance learning, rural education, and personnel preparation.

Notes